You've got it made, Snoopy

Selected cartoons from
YOU'VE HAD IT CHARLIE BROWN,
VOLUME 1

Charles M. Schulz

CORONET BOOKS
Hodder Fawcett, London

First published 1974 by
Fawcett Publications Inc.

Coronet edition 1975
Fifth impression 1978

Printed in Great Britain for
Hodder Fawcett Ltd., Mill Road, Dunton Green,
Sevenoaks, Kent (Editorial Office:
47 Bedford Square, London, WC1 3DP) by
C. Nicholls & Company Ltd,
The Philips Park Press, Manchester

ISBN 0 340 19550 9

HERE'S THE WORLD-FAMOUS HOCKEY PLAYER WINDING UP FOR ONE OF HIS SPECTACULAR SLAP SHOTS...

POW!

SOME PEOPLE HAVE DOGS WHO BARK TOO MUCH... SOME PEOPLE HAVE DOGS WHO CHASE CHICKENS... SOME PEOPLE HAVE DOGS WHO DIG UP FLOWERS...

"GREAT SHOT!" THANK YOU, STAN... THANK YOU, BOBBY... THANK YOU, MAURICE...

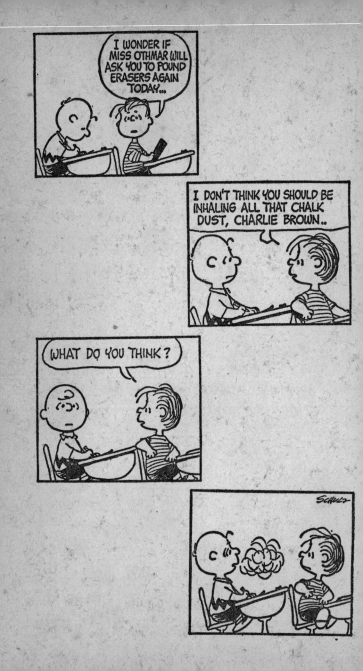

JOGGING IS MY THING!

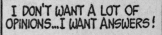

THE WONDERFUL WORLD OF PEANUTS

Numbers 1-25 and all the above Peanuts titles are available at your local bookshop or newsagent, or can be ordered direct from the publisher Just tick the titles you want and fill in the form below.
Prices and availability subject to change without notice.

CORONET BOOKS, P.O. Box 11, Falmouth, Cornwall.
Please send cheque or postal order, and allow the following for postage and packing:
U.K.—One book 22p plus 10p per copy for each additional book ordered, up to a maximum of 82p.
B.F.P.O. and EIRE—22p for the first book plus 10p per copy for the next 6 books, thereafter 4p per book.

OTHER OVERSEAS CUSTOMERS—30p for the first book and 10p per copy for each additional book.

Name ....

Address ....

....